DON'T

F- - -

WITH

LOVE

Master Love and Be Forever Young, Like me at 78

Sally D. Preston

ISBN: 978-1-7378316-0-0 (paperback)

978-1-7378316-1-7 (hardback)

978-1-7378316-2-4 (ebook)

Dedication

TO MY GRANDCHILDREN, Joshua, Lauren and Jackson, who truly brought out extraordinary love and joy pouring out of me that I didn't know was possible. Forever Thank You. And, to their Mother, Tracey Deanne, my one and only, who after bringing her into life through me, gave to me, through her support, challenges, inspiration, and most of all her sacred existence, a reason, purpose and the strength to CHARGE relentlessly through my own life.

Contents

Acknowledgments

THANKS TO MY family for loving and supporting me and listening to my never ending excitement over all my new endeavors and ventures and never ending excessive talking and accepting me even when they didn't agree or understand me. Big thanks to the brilliant Jackson Wagener for single-handedly taking my mess of a manuscript and converting it into the perfect book format in order to send to the publisher and print. To Jane Hufstedler, who inspired me into remembering who I am and to find my voice. Thanks to Karyn Hunter for her steadfast faith, encouragement and all her gifts of love and acknowledgment. And, for all the hours she spent reading and listening to all my training videos and proof readings of this book. And, most of all, being such a positive force in my life. Thank you also to Karen Drucker and her miraculous healing music that not only healed my life physically, mentally and spiritually also inspired me during my writing of this book and because of her guidance in her workshop that led me to believe I could have my own Podcast. And a big thank you to Sarah Cordiner and her genius for teaching how to have your own online courses, writing your own book and 100's of other courses. This book for sure, literally, would not have been possible without her and her extraordinary, explicit training And thank you to all those beautiful lightworkers and doctors, physicists and experts that I listen to and have helped me evolve into the being and knowing spirit that I came here to be. In my List To Enlightenment and Transformation, I have mentioned many of you. On my Podcast, I will mention and introduce many more. And thanks to all my clients that have given me so much knowledge, inspiration and understanding and have for sure proven to me that you teach what you have to learn. And, last but not least, Pam Sanchez, who gave me two blank composition books, labeled Book 1 and Book 2, over 20 years ago. I filled in the blank pages of those to write this book. Thank you.

Introduction

IT'S ABSOLUTELY AMAZING to me that all of a sudden after almost two years of my Life Coach Certification and over $75,000 in training and classes and over 30,000 hours in training, I still have not launched my business in a really consistent committed way. I spent three months and thousands of $$ in training to set up my own on-line course which was free and my intention was to just build my client base. I sent out a couple posts on Facebook and one paid campaign and I have ten or fifteen people who signed in to take my course and now are automatically in my Active Campaign System which I had intended to build so that I would eventually have a base to enroll clients into my membership program and potential listeners for my podcast. And, the PodCast is my main goal and above all I want to create.

I was so hung up on learning all the technology to launch, build my list, learn how to do a podcast that I pretty much wore myself out and almost lost interest in my entire goal and dream. On top of all that, I've been writing a book for over two years that I thought would be a good idea to launch first before I did my podcast to enlarge my audience and interest for my podcast. I truly feel (I am definitely a feeler) I have a mission and purpose and I KNOW I am here right now on this earth plane to fulfill that purpose. Unfortunately, there has been something that has been keeping me from taking action to fulfill that purpose, launch the business, finish the book, and create the podcast.

I am here to support others in their transition and transformation in higher consciousness. I know that and up until now, I haven't been clear exactly what my speciality and modality would be to do that. The thing that was holding me back though was a fear of being too much and doing too much. First, being too much was a lifetime issue with me in my family. I talked too much, I worked too much, I spent too much, I was just overall too much and would tend to over do everything and take responsibility for the happiness of everyone I was involved with. So, in order to please, help, support others, which is what Empaths are here to do, I felt I needed to be less than in order for others to feel good about themselves. I have a very unique gift. I used to say it was I see the GOOD in others and also what they are talented at and/or their strengths. This helped them follow through on their own purpose and goals in their lives. Now I realize I was seeing GOD in others And, what a perfect time in our evolution to be able to do this. So, why couldn't I get busy and get out there and launch my business, finish the book and do that podcast??? All of the hours and days and months I spent learning all the technical expertise, I realize now was only a diversion and causing resistance, which always keeps you from your goals and dreams. What does all this have to do with YOU? Stay with me and it will all come together for you. I love that because not only will IT all come together by the end of this book there is a chance we can ALL come together.

COURAGE IS FEAR WALKING not the ABSENCE of fear. Someone said that in one of the 1,000 books I've read. I do tend to exaggerate, although this isn't an exaggeration. And, I always write things down that impress or inspire me. I then think I will use it in one of my classes or writing for OTHERS. I do this alot or used to until recently. I would see an article, listen to YouTube inspirational or self transformational information and think of everyone who NEEDS to listen or read it. I finally realized and it was just recently for God sakes, that No-one but me needs to hear or see this whatever it is. It is for Me and ONLY me that is why I was drawn to it or it was drawn to me. I learned there may be times I may be inspired to share something with others and I have found that will happen when I have asked in prayer or meditation, how or what would someone need to move forward or for their highest good. Then if something pops up that fits my request for the other person, then it is safe to share. Other than that in most cases, I am interfering with their growth instead of helping or contributing. All of the focus on saving, healing, finding fault with, fear for their destructive behavior is just a diversion from my/our own issues and dealing with my/ our own pain and self destructive ways. I stop myself now when I want to offer solutions, direction or YouTube videos and then ask myself Why do I think they need this? How can I know what someone else needs? I then ask myself how I can utilize the information and ALWAYS something comes to me. I am a Life Coach and many times I have had this urgency to give direction to one or more of my clients of what they need to do. There are times if they have asked me that I may give them a certain direction or meditation, and then, only, after I have taken this advice and questioned myself. This happened recently when I was working with a client who was in an abusive relationship that I could see was escalating. Some of the things I wanted her to do for her own safety and peace, I realized first, I needed to do things in my own relationships that I was thinking she should do. What is vital when you are "helping" others and especially if you are in the health, and/or coaching business and serving others, is to turn it back to them to contemplate, question within and come up with their own answer. The answer is always within. People who have made extraordinary transformations and healings and are believing it was me or any other coach, teacher that did the healing and then becoming dependent on them, is not the way to go. I am the bridge, funnel or pointer. True success comes from within yourself. If you believe you are getting the comfort and changes because of someone else and you are attached to them, if they aren't available when you have a challenge or question, then you will tend to fall back to before your healing and/or transformation. Learn to rely on yourself to make the changes necessary and feel the fear and do it anyway. That is what it means by courage is fear walking.

This is so hard to understand, like loving yourself. What does that mean and how do you do that? Loving yourself begins with learning to trust yourself and listen to yourself. Self soothe without any outside influence, drugs, alcohol, sex or even another person or animal. These outside answers may soothe or satisfy you for the moment and then when something happens and you don't have access to any of the things that helped you soothe or complete yourself in the past and you have already formed the habit and belief this was your go-to helper, then things start falling apart in your life. Confidence plummets, depression may set in and it is like a drug you are withdrawing from unless you realize that everything you are looking for outside is within you.

Not to worry. I will give you the PROVEN tools and exercises to find that place within with all the answers and a way to self soothe and feel safe . Remember, it's not outside, it's not the government, it's not the democrats, it's not the republicans, its not the men or the women, it's not the black, blue, white, yellow whatever other difference or nationality, it's not the people who wear or not wear a mask. It is something inside of you that needs to heal and be released. IT'S NOT YOUR FAULT EITHER AND YOU ARE NOT BROKEN. If you would like, in the meantime, to instantly soothe and release stress and even reduce your blood pressure, check out these short energy exercises on my YouTube channel. https:// youtube.com/channel/UCPm2Y4XElgyRUooHGz5jJDw and/or look for Sally Preston.

One

Stop Your Overthinking

REALLY? IT'S REALLY close to impossible to tell yourself
to stop thinking about anything. It's like the old story about
going into a room and sitting in a corner and NOT thinking of a pink elephant. Then, of course, that's all you think
about no matter how hard you try not to. What you can do
more effectively is practice to change and be aware of what
you are thinking about, not Stop thinking. Why would we
want to stop thinking? Would you want to have your heart
stop beating? Or, your lungs stop breathing? Of course not,
so why stop thinking. It's good to think. Just start by being
aware of WHAT you are thinking about. If all of a sudden

you are feeling an emotion either sadness, weakness, tiredness, anger, stop and ask yourself what was I thinking of? As soon as you pinpoint the thought , ask yourself is this something that is happening right now? Do I need to think or resolve this right now? Then, again, say to yourself, and it's important you either talk out loud or silently to yourself. For instance, say, Beautiful mind or Sweetheart or Buddy, it's not necessary to deal with this now. Maybe next week or maybe it is never even going to happen. Just give your mind PERMISSION to let it go. It's vitally important if you want this to work, that you actually speak to your mind directly as though it was an entity sitting right there before you. It will take your instruction exactly as you say it and FEEL it. It will do whatever you requested. Just like keying a program into a computer., or talking to Alexa. It is that part of your mind that is conscious only and only can perform according to what you and society have programmed into it. When you become aware and observe a thought that you just had and give it a new order/program, you are coming from a higher part of your mind that really knows everything you need to do and is with you always and always has been and can create anything you want. Because its only job is to give the instructions to your mind and recode for your highest good. Let us try it right now on something small. No doubt your mind is going/running strong and probably something that you are worrying about. If not, think of something that you have been worrying about. Stop and really concentrate on it. For example, you are worrying, dreading your talkative, negative neighbor might pop in as she sometimes does and you definitely don't want that now. So, say to yourself something supportive like, I know you don't need this now and you really don't know she is coming tonight and really even if she does it's not the end of the world. I give you permission to just tell her you really need to be alone and rest now and then say something kind to her like, I am always wishing you the best and that only good comes your way, just need to take care of me tonight. And, then end the thought process with saying it probably isn't going to happen and if it does, I KNOW what to do and how to handle it, so no need to worry. Name It! Face It! Resolve It! Create the scenario for whatever your dread or problem is. There are no problems in God and or the Universe, only solutions. We create the problems, not believing the solution is already out there, so we don't see it, since we are only focusing on the problem that we created out of fear or instinct in our minds.

All of this is explained in detail in the book "You're Not Broken 5 Steps to become Superconscious" by Christopher Michael Duncan. I highly recommend for you to witness five steps that normally would take years to work through, resolve and learn, that Chris teaches you how to learn to release instantaneously, especially trauma. It works and lasts too for most, a lifetime. Amazingly, the particular fear, pain whatever that you released and re-coded is gone forever and won't come up again. Things that you think you have worked through and just keep surfacing again and then you think, I can't believe this is coming up again; I thought I had already dealt with it. What you may have done in the past was recognize the fear or pain, whatever it was and even may have re-lived it. What you probably didn't do was recode and release it. Without doing this, the pain, hurt, whatever, will resurface automatically when something triggers it. You may not even know what happened. If something causes you to automatically feel anger, fear, revenge and it just comes on without you thinking any of it beforehand, then this is your sign, it's a trauma emotion that is still inside your body./mind . It turns out , every cell in our body has memory, not just the cells in our brain. Most of what you are unknowingly still holding on to is in the mind.

In this writing, I am giving you easy, just to try, exercises and then when you prove to yourself it works and you want to master this; then Duncan's book and/or classes will do that. I have attended live classes, studied and read 100's of books on this subject, which were great and helped me incorporate pieces into my life little by little. Duncan's book, however, is written in such an easy to read format and makes it easier to understand why we have found ourselves in repeated and painful situations and a proven way to move out of and finally stay centered and self reliant that lasts and gets you to a life that you love every single moment of every day. No matter what is going on externally and in the world. That is where I am now. Duncan's and other training and especially this book helped me find those left over pieces that I wasn't even aware of that were keeping me from finishing my book, launching my business and starting my podcast. Now with all that said , only read his book because it is resonating or calling to you and feels like something you are really wanting to dive into. Not because I recommended it. That goes for everything I recommend or believe in that I talk about in this book. What doesn't resonate with you, just disregard it. Use your free will and be open at the same time to new things that may be something that is right for you at this time, or not. You choose.

Go to YouTube

Christopher Duncan Life Recode Experience Training for example of the recode process he does and is explained in his book.

Two
Are You Trying to Control the World?

ARE YOU TRYING to control your's or your family's outcome in a situation? Are you trying to control anything for that matter because you really don't have any control over your own life; let alone anyone else's. What you can do though for your own peace of mind and good will is put yourself and your mind in joyful, peaceful, loving situations because you may not be able to change others, you can control how you react to others and the world. How do you do that, you ask? I can only tell you what I have done through

COVID, the election, masks, no masks, killings all over the world including my own neighborhood, climate change, vaccine demands, and other things that may have come up that were disturbing and or what may come up in the future.

The very first thing I would do if you wanted to release a big piece of stress is refrain from listening to mainstream news all day, fear based, brainwashing, programming, tell you who and what to like or don't like News. All of it Liberal/ Conservative with radical angry talking heads on the major stations that the majority of the world is listening to now. I have to hand it to the major all day news programs, that they used brilliant marketing tactics to get and keep their audience. For starters, telling everyone how stupid everyone else was who didn't listen to them and stressing how vital it was that you BE INFORMED. I always thought even back in the beginning when I kept hearing people say, I want to be informed. They had their everyday audience really believing that they had to stay informed and the only one that could inform them was that particular station. Listening to other stations was almost a crime. It reminded me of the catholic church. We had to go to church every sunday or it was a sin and we were forbidden to ever go to a non-catholic church. I have stayed informed by listening to my local news and weather every night at 5pm and National right after. I always hear the main things going on all over the world and more importantly what is major in my own home town or state. I listened to all the COVID updates daily, which they had and called Facts without Fear. Also, I listen to the speeches that our President or Governor gives live at the time and hear what they really said, not an excerpt or out of context clip depending on what station and politics the mainstream news or social media is pushing. I also listened to the COVID updates from our governor which were live almost daily at first and now, as of this writing weekly. I learned to trust him and felt that he was making his decisions not on a political bias . I believe that he made decisions on what he truly believed was the best for our state and all those concerned and the facts that he brought in from research and experts and still made decisions on what he thought was best. Above all I refused to fear anything or anyone or especially COVID. Fear is like a magnet and I refuse to accept it into my life. I washed my hands much more, stayed happily in my home creating and learning, and took my vitamin D and Tumeric and used extreme self care. That keeps your immune system strong. Listening to my local news and getting to know the news and weather people and knowing they only report the news and do not tell me their opinion or who is right or wrong or who to hate, brings me peace and joy and at the same time I think I am totally informed in what I need to know. I then get to choose what I want for myself and my world in my own mind. Keep that thought, not what someone on the news tells me is happening and going to happen especially if it is scaring me and others. I'm very particular about what I want to be informed of and it's mostly things that are vast and I may not fully understand and it holds my attention and inspires me at the same time educating me in things that expand my mind and consciousness in wondrous and miraculous ways. I may not come across real smart and up to date on all the political ups and downs; I am however feeling more and more conscious and self aware and wise and still at total peace within myself. So that's why I don't watch FOX, CNN or CNBC or any of those political social media shows. Again, it's fine if you do watch them. There is definitely nothing wrong with it. I know brilliant and kind and loving people who listen every day. Just be aware, if it's upsetting you or setting your mind in an area you really don't feel is who you are and if you feel afraid after hearing what someone is telling you, then maybe take a break and get your breath back and listen to what your true self is trying to tell you so you will really be informed from a higher source.

Another practice I have is I don't judge and do not believe in categorizing people. Why is the media saying the democrats are this and the republicans are that? Half the things they say that are the democrats or the republicans fault really are not even the majority of either party feelings or opinions on whatever the subject is. Again, it really truly is what station you listen to in order to find out who is really to blame and who is wrong and now evil. This just isn't in the United States, where I am; it is all over the world. Again, the problem is not the liberals or the conservatives, the real problem is the lower energy force behind them both that is wanting to take over the world and in order to do that, they have to separate us. Now I know this is tending to sound like a conspiracy theory which could be true or not. Some of it I do not at all believe, especially when they are bringing in fear and promoting violence. I do not believe in censoring those that are questioning some of the tactics that are in place to take away our freedom and censor us from hearing or learning things from so-called conspiracy leaders. For example, Bill Icke, you can believe him or not, but we deserve the right to make up our own minds and not censor him so we can't listen. Icke, right or wrong, has pretty much spent half his life researching and gathering information which can in many cases be proven correct. I completely agree that we must start questioning many of the things we are being told and mandated to do. I truly believe we must keep our sovereignty and speak our truth. And, give others the same right. I do not believe that in order to win and keep our sovereignty and speak our truth, we must attack, verbally abuse and even kill our fellow man when they don't believe what we do. Again, they are only acting out and believing what they were taught to believe or act out from their family and society of origin and what media they choose to listen to in the present time. Those against anyone, especially to fear and hate them, could have easily been born in their country or religion and then would be acting out in the same way that they have been taught and programmed. We all need to start questioning the beliefs that have been instilled in us and whether or not we are sure that is our truth. I saw on the news (main local/ national channel 10) the other night where people on airplanes are beating up on flight attendants because they are insisting that they wear masks and in some cases or maybe just one, because they didn't want to wear a seat belt. It showed attendants with bloody faces from attacks from the passengers over the mandate to wear masks. Now it could be, it was all fake and really didn't happen, however, since I kept hearing it was happening on different airlines it seemed possibly true. And, I have to say the behavior again on both sides for masks and no masks has been annoying and mean to say the least. I do not think we should be forced to wear masks overall as a law and I do believe it's part of the conspiracy to see how much THEY can get control of us along with the NRA and Big Pharma . I do believe that COVID is real and regardless of where it started, I think it also was part of a plan to spread fear so broadly and on top of that bring back the pharmaceutical companies as the hero to solve the pandemic and save the world and God only knows how many vaccinations will be needed the rest of our lives which may or may not have harmful chemicals or whatever in it, that changes our DNA. And, God only knows what else that again plays into and supports the Take Over the World plan. Regardless , if this is true or not and the last thing we want to do if we do believe it's true is to FEAR. That is the one thing THEY know will give them the power if we buy into fear and do ,what they want us to do more than anything, is FEAR and by the way tell us who and what to fear. Again, speaking your truth and keeping your sovereignty and saying NO to taking away your rights, does not mean beating up and attacking the airline attendant asking you to abide by the rules of her/his company, which she or he must do themselves whether they like it or not. In this case, the passengers get to take their masks off once they reach their destinations and the flight attendants may have another two or three more flights that they have to keep wearing their masks. I heard from a friend that someone on one of the news channels, was telling their listeners after it was announced that masks didn't have to be worn outside, and they demanded to their listeners, that if they saw anyone , even a child , with a parent, wearing a mask that they go up and tell the parent to take it off and that it is child abuse. Now, if this did occur and as ridiculous as that sounds and if you did hear this and believe it, just know the same kind of warnings and threats are going out on the other stations who attack those people in public places, like grocery stores etc, because they are NOT wearing a mask. I saw this on Dr. Phil. The lady who got attacked in the grocery store for not wearing a mask and she had called ahead of time and got permission because of an allergy or some medical problem. I'm 78 and have had pneumonia four times and I really refused to be afraid of COVID for all the reasons I have given. Since I really didn't listen to any political station, I wasn't aware at first that there was a mask no mask issue. Frankly, I would have been fine wearing a mask. I just was very clear I did not want it to be a law to wear one. Then that would open up along with several other stupid laws, just more law suits and suing each other and attorneys making tons of money and yet another way to divide us. Als0, I am not against attorneys. There are plenty of brilliant, purpose filled for the good of mankind out there.

My sister is one of them and is also a Federal Judge her most favorite part of her most worthy and responsible position is to hold the Naturalized American Citizen Oath ceremony, which is a tradition dating back to the 18th century. I went to one and cried when I listened to and saw the pride and joy of all these immigrants becoming Americans. Not to digress, and back to the mask issue, if there had not been that wear or don't wear mask and you are good or bad media going on, I don't believe there would have really been any big problem to wearing a mask. I also did not fall into the trap that it's someone else's fault or negligence if they don't wear a mask, or get the shot, or whatever and someone like me gets sick. No one else is responsible for my health. I will either just not go out, which is what I did, and or keep wearing a mask even if I don't have to. That's another way to separate us, is to blame the other and make people feel guilty. We are in a divide bigger than ever only because that is the plan and the tactics to keep us separate through the media. THEY are behind both arguments. Like Double Agents, they direct the media to gang up on those who wear masks and then THEY go right over to the other side and give the orders to gang up on those who won't wear masks, again through the media. I heard on a YouTube interview the other day and I do not remember who said it and I have not researched as he said to verify the truth. He said that there is a media representative of every major broadcast station on the board of every phar-maceutical company except CVS, who sits on the board and takes back whatever information they need to share for the benefit of the Pharma company and then makes that the news and what is being told to the public as truth. I didn't research it, because this makes perfect sense to me because I just knew intuitively it was happening. I just didn't know how the information was getting there. Don't believe me, do your own research. I absolutely could be wrong. Just be aware and question what you hear to be true. Especially, when they tell you it's the only truth.

Three
What Can We Do?

STARTING WITH OURSELVES, instead of beating up the airline attendant. Go within yourself and contemplate and ask what you as an individual can do to keep our sovereignty and help this earth and all on it, evolve to the next dimension. And, find out ways you can actually experience not only peace of mind, also heaven on earth. That I know is a big fat contemplation and you may not be contemplating any ideas on how to help the collective move to a higher dimension and leave this matrix behind, but as soon as you do start asking and contemplating ideas will flow. Also, many scientists are saying the movie The Matrix is more like a documentary than a fiction movie. We are all energy, pure energy and all of us are connected. As we evolve, we learn more of what is true and what is real. Love is the only answer. When you come back at any danger or threat with love, it completely changes not only you but anyone and everything around you. Fear sets you back, takes all your power and keeps you in the lower levels of life and makes you vulnerable for someone or something to come in and take every ounce of freedom from you. Once you have practiced loving whatever arises and extraordinary trusting and loving yourself first, and then learning to be present with others regardless of their beliefs, then there will be too many of us so strong and so filled up with the ammunition of love, nothing or no one can take away our freedom or peace of mind or prosperity. Just keep practicing loving and believing in yourself that you are more powerful than any outside force. Be kind to those still struggling and are afraid. It is so important not to judge or argue or force your opinions on anyone else. They can't help it and have been programmed to believe,it's the other, to fear or blame. Just becoming enlightened, awake and aware and keeping yourself in a state of peace, makes you sooooo powerful that those around you can change too. Not their opinions, just their way of being in joy, peace and love instead of fear. You keep speaking your truth without violence of any kind and let others have their own beliefs and freedom of speech without violence. Everyone has the right to their own beliefs no matter how different it may seem to you. Remember they, like you, were born perfect and then taught whatever language, beliefs their parents and community programmed into them. You also could hve been born in France and spoke French or in Islam or grew up as Muslim or whatever you were taught. Why blame, condemn or fear or try to change anyone's behavior when they are only acting out their own beliefs that they were taught. Acceptance and respect will be what changes them because deep down, all everyone wants is to love and be loved. Everyone is here to follow their own path. All paths lead back to God/Source. Next flight or public trip of any kind that you go on with a group of others and conflict arises over anything especially now the current mask/no mask situation . Just comply with a feeling inside of freedom and acceptance and know that no one is taking your freedom from you unless you give it away. You do not give your power away if you choose to wear a mask during the flight, what is it going to hurt if you get all frantic,upset and angry.You keep your power because you are choosing to wear the mask and stay totally at peace. What we need to expose is the establishments that are trying to control and divide us and force laws that take our freedom away and then we do it by standing up and speaking our truth in a nonviolent way. So, back to your plane trip, bring a feeling of love sooo strong into your heart and then expand that love throughout the entire location of where you are and watch all the people around you settle down in a peaceful, calm, even fun atmosphere. Don't knock it till you try it. I just did it on my recent flight to California and all was perfect. It does take your practice for your own self awareness and trust and love; so it would be a gift to yourself to keep practicing on yourself and become a Master of bringing light and peace wherever you go. Remember UNITED we win. DIVIDED we fall. The enemy is not you or me or the flight attendants. Nothing can take us over if we do not divide, shame, blame and fear each other. Even the so-called enemy does not need to be feared. Staying in the high vibration of love stops the so-called negative/lower entity in its tracks. Like the crucifix with the Vampire!!

Right now the greatest thing you can do for mankind, along with first learning to love and trust yourself, is to release and dissolve all the low vibrations of hate, resentment, regret and most of all fear! For God sakes 75-80% of this world is being told the only thing that will save you and your family is to have a gun to protect yourself. How on earth can this be the only solution?? What do you think is REALLY behind this epidemic to have a gun and carry it because you have to protect yourself from almost everyone. OMG, I saw this ad pop up on the internet from US Concealed Online. It said Get Your Concealed Gun Carry Certification Today!! Are you kidding me? People are getting carry certifications online? The Ad also said Hurry. Get Certified before Anti-Gun Groups shut this down! How can this be legal? I wonder how much it costs to get one and who/what is behind this? It makes sense to believe that it's necessary to protect ourselves and carry a gun and I know and love several people who do believe it. However, it only takes believing something to drive you to create that reality. . And , what again do you think caused this extraordinary plunge into fear and passion to have to carry a gun? Ask yourself, why do I want/need to have a gun to carry with me. Keep asking why at least four times. Write down each answer. You may be surprised if you don't have a real valid reason, except fear, which has been programmed into you by others acting for or the NRA and the innate programmed fear of the world outside that was programmed into us since childhood. All the shootings now going on in the underprivileged neighborhoods are again based on guns are the answer and they have been brought up in conditions that never reflected or taught them nor had they ever experienced a life in peace, love and prosperity. Most kids grew up only knowing drugs, sexual, physical abuse, crime as everyday life and no one to show them the way. The ones who did come from those kinds of environments and got out, always had at least one person who helped them find their love and purpose. It only takes one. I saw an older movie recently with Paul Newman called Somebody up there Likes me. It was based on Rocky Graciano's life. He was always in trouble as a kid and was growing up in a similar environment as I described above. He was in jail when someone took interest in him and noticed his talent for fighting and trained him and believed in him and completely changed his life. Great movie. Don't know if all of it was true, but the main theme is that people's lives can change . It only takes one person and I believe God /Universe works through that person and miracles happen. Maybe you could be that one person for someone.

Einstein said the most important question you can ever ask yourself is; Do I live in a safe or dangerous world? Because whatever you believe is what you will see

Four

How to Use the Power of Love

HOW DO YOU think you can use this power? Believe it or not you start by loving YOURSELF. I have found from my own experience that this is the one major habit we have to practice in order to reach that peace of mind we are looking for. No-one tells you that growing up because no-one ever told the people who were teaching us. The only thing we really ever learn to even like about ourselves is what we DO. Did we get good grades? Did we work hard? (Big One for me) Did we look good, perfect skin, perfect weight? Did we help others and sacrifice our own needs? Even to the point of exhaustion or becoming sick. Were we a good boy or good

girl and always behave in public, never speak out or dis-
agree? Did we always respect and never question authority?
Again, this was a big one for me being brought up catholic
and in catholic schools till my senior year. And the more
you deprive yourself the more you are that coveted "good"
person and never asking for what you want (even in prayers).

I have realized in the past couple years that even though I
have truly loved others and worked hard and forgave everyone , no matter what; I unfortunately really never loved
myself or even took care of myself. I only knew how to take
care of others. When I was so sick with pneumonia (four
times), I realized I didn't know how to take care of myself.
That's probably why I had pneumonia four times, slow learn-
er. I can say now, I truly know how to take care of myself
and of course, that starts with loving yourself. It changed
everything. Not only my health; also my relationships. I
finally learned from the originator of the Love Revolution,
Matt Kahn, how to love myself and how vital it is to not only
to learn how to love yourself but then also realize you must
love yourself FIRST before anyone and everything. Here is
why. It's impossible to truly love another if you don't have it
inside you to give. In order to change the world, we first have
to love ourselves which heals everything within us that is
causing all the fear and hate and regret.

Being an empath, I was only thinking of loving others and
literally taking on their pain FOR them. They would leave
feeling better and I would come down sick! Matt taught
Empaths how to be kind and patient with others AND get

the space to focus and love ourselves through any criticism or outward attacks from another. You can find Matt Kahn on YouTube easily; just type in his name. He has life changing talks and if you do go to YouTube to find him, the exact talk or program will come up for you and exactly what you need to hear at the moment. That's how this stuff works. Also, I've read all his books and much of the information I had never heard before and I have been in self help and spiritual learning for over 50 years. For me, being an Empath, I was always doing the "good" person routine and always putting others first, even when in abusive relationships. Matt helps you learn to put yourself first and give yourself the support and love and understanding and at the same time, maintaining and giving the love and support to others. Basically, it's taking time out with loving thoughts and communicating with others, that you just need to take care of "Me" now. All bets are off though in abusive relationships. There are no compromises. Just leave and protect and love yourself more. Once you focus on protecting and loving yourself more, there are no more abusive relationships in your life. Again, you correct your thinking, if you do this as I did, that the other person will change if you just love them more; that does not ever work. Only when you love yourself more, does anything or anyone else change. I will put a list of Matt's Books at the end of this book. Following the exercises and learning more and more ways to love yourself, which I will give you in this book, just may make you feel inside so safe that you won't need or want to carry your gun anymore. Which has nothing to do with gun control. I have no problem with people having guns. What doesn't make sense to me is all the advertising that gun control groups are trying to take your guns away and the big deal over the 2nd Amendment. I hear of laws trying to be passed for restrictions on those war automatic guns and for criminals or people who should not have them due to mental illness. Again, depending who you listen to, it's being said and sold especially by the NRA that your guns are going to be taken away. That was all started to scare everyone and have them stock up on guns, which many did which really made the NRA happy. Again, controlling through fear. We don't need gun laws by the government. What we really need is to stop killing each other and start trusting each other and teach our kids to trust and love without fear. I know, how can you do that in today's world with all the anger, shootings and killings. You can learn to love yourself and fear dissipates and then it's easy to teach your kids because you will have experienced the changes you have made in your reality and world just by learning to love yourself and spreading it throughout your dominion.

Five

Everything is Happening For You Not to You

IF YOU ARE still with me and still curious, then the chances are you are ready to make some changes in your life. You may even start questioning whether your beliefs and opinions are the only way of thinking and better yet, that your beliefs are not the only truth. If that is you, then you will start seeing a completely new reality in your world. When your thoughts and beliefs change, your life and world around you changes. And, if you still aren't convinced that you can do anything to change your world or yourself and just don't want to or don't agree with anything I've said so far, that is fine. There is nothing wrong with that. Wherever you are right now, it is just right for you and you are exactly where you are supposed to be. No matter what it looks like to others or even yourself. You are not wrong. You are exactly in the relationship, job, home, location that you will learn whatever it is that you, personally, need/want to learn and experience. Having the experience is the only way you can really learn. That's why the old saying about not judging until we walk in someone else's shoes is so true. We have no idea what they have experienced and then programmed into their mind and then it became their belief system and was automatically running them. I heard just today, someone referring to the belief system as BS. I love that and described it perfectly. We all have our BS and none of it is true, even though for us we passionately do believe it is true. Just like religion. It depends on what family you were born into and how you were raised in what it is you believe and then argue with people because you believe your BS is the right way and others are wrong. Right now in our current state of affairs, in order for us to have our sovereignty and peace of mind, we have to learn how to UNLEARN everything we know now.

What I am attempting to do in this book is give you a crash course and literally a Heimlich Maneuver, to get you into the safe and peaceful state that you deserve . No matter who you are or what you have done. When you clean out and release all those traumatic and painful thoughts and beliefs and per- ceived right and wrongs in your past, you completely cleanse your soul and wipe everything clean and move forward free and with a new passion for your life. In the Catholic religion, we would go to confession and we were told since first grade that once you went to confession your sins were forgiven. That really was a great belief for children because then after confession, you truly believed whatever you had done was forgiven..The only thing is, it also taught us that only the Priest in the confessional can give you absolution and forgiveness; which is not true. We were led to believe we couldn't get forgiveness from God on our own. There are plenty of non-catholics that pray and ask forgiveness from God and have that feeling of truly being forgiven. God is not keeping score of your perceived rights and wrongs or good or bad. What is wrong in one religion or culture is perfectly right in another. Again, it depends, where you were born and what family. We Catholics were also taught about sin, venial and mortal, and if you die with a mortal sin on your soul, you go straight to hell. That is why the Sacrament, Last Rights is so important to have by a priest at your deathbed. Now, really, do you believe God would set up the venial and mortal sin system? Besides, the true meaning of Sin and translated definition is missing the mark. Missing the mark to me. should NOT be grounds to send you to hell. That is just one of the millions of beliefs going through our minds and unconsciously running the show, which causes other negative and fearful thoughts to come up consciously and constantly in our day to day lives. No wonder we have trouble sleeping at night and why we are walking through our lives like zombies and asleep during the day. Hopefully, this information will start your awakening if you haven't already woken up. I'm just giving information that can start or further wake you. Detailed and thorough information, from the experts I will refer you to at the end of this book. I also am giving you tools to use right now to help you through the hard times when you don't want or have time to study the scientific and spiritual master's teachings. And most importantly, don't think I know what's right for you, because I don't and don't believe what I say either. It is what worked for me. Only try it ,if you want for yourself ,and then decide. All information coming to you from everywhere, it would be best to think critically about every story and piece of information we hear or read. And speaking of forgiveness like as in love, we first have to forgive ourselves before we can genuinely forgive another.

While digital communications have created a global village in which we're all interconnected, it has also divided us into our own information silos. Our natural reactions to the uncertainty we've been experiencing might also be exacerbating the issue, particularly when it comes to conspiracy theories. We're conditioned to find stories that explain what's going on around us. Fueling the situation, every time you click on a story or advertisement, you leave electronic footprints the internet uses to determine what information will pop up on your screen next time you're browsing. So our online activities create this bubble, so we see information that reinforces our worldview and of course our own belief system (BS). Thus building up info true or untrue to reinforce our position and divide with those who don't agree with us. Barbara Fister, a media literacy expert and professor emerita at Gustavus Adolphus College gives these points on how to navigate the search for trustworthy information. Who created the content? Who wrote and published it? Red flags: no byline and/or the source is an organization you can't verify. How is the information presented? Is it a reported article with quotes? Are there exaggerations? Is it an ad or donation request? What points of view are represented? How is the story framed? How might other people react or interpret it differently?

I have been very alert to whatever I hear or read. Some of the conspiracy theories I may take in as new information, I wasn't aware of, especially the stuff about the aliens. I was never interested before in any of the alien stories, sightings whatsoever. Really, never gave it any thought of whether they were real or not. Now after listening to Gaia and other information from Archeologists, I think I AM ONE!! And, my family and maybe you by now, thinks I may be too. I've really never fit in except now with opening up and expanding my awareness and learning, I have a network of supportive people that help me feel more like I belong. I had to learn on my own though, that I belong wherever I am or I would not be there. When I am listening or reading anything I'm not sure of, I go by what I feel. If someone is saying this is the only way and if what they say is causing fear, then I choose not to take it in. Even if there are things that are happening in the world that are fearful and destructive, I look for the solution and or what I can do to help or change the outcome. It's always keeping your focus on love, being nonjudgmental, and totally trust in God/Source that all is in Divine Order.

I stated at the beginning of the book that I was so caught up in all the outside interference and unknown resistance within myself, that I could not move forward in my Coaching Business, finishing my book and my ultimate dream of having a unique and highly transformational Podcast. Now I am inspired and on auto pilot and am in flow to complete and publish this book as an urgent call to action for mankind 's freedom and sovereignty. According to astrology and the predictions of the Aztec Indians, beginning on May 26, 2021 and lasting until June 10,2021 there will be an influx of divine energy and activation for those who are in the higher vibration of Love. Just a neutral/medium state will do it. In order to receive this activation, we must completely leave behind regret, hate and especially fear. I choose to believe in this and so I am doing the best I can to help everyone who wants it, to forgive everyone and everything, especially yourself and love greater than ever before. In fact, this is the code and the solution if you are wanting to evolve to the next dimension and with the earth, who is going with or without us. That's what all of the huge changes in the world are about. The earth is evolving and it has happened several times before. I won't get into the physics and science here and I couldn't explain it like the Scientists and Physics Experts do. You can if you like, start your own research and also check out the interviews and shows on Gaia and the History channel. I don't need any more proof. I'm focusing on what I learned from all my research and studies. The solution is as I said before, forgive everyone and everything, especially yourself and love greater than ever before. Here is a practice tool. Just pretend; make a picture in your imagination where the world is at peace and in only love. Picture it in your own way. Marvel at your power and always know God/Source knows and is ONLY DIVINE ORDER. You can do the vision to start with for your day at the office or a meeting you are dreading and then move on to the world. When you do and it happens, you feel so great and then have more faith to do it more often. A great quote by Einstein is "Imagination is the preview of Coming Attractions". So see, I'm not just making this stuff up. I just want to share with you the infinite possibilities that you have access to, because I Love You!!!! Yes, YOU. I really do. It's a feeling I've had while writing this book as if it is a letter to my dearest loved ones. That's what happens when you learn to come from your heart instead of your head, which comes as you learn to love yourself.

A way to do that is in Matt Kahn's book "Love What Is" . No matter what or who it is; first accept/love whatever is before you. Then ask within, for what action to take if any. Start with simple things until you get the hang of it. Maybe you have a tight place in the back of your neck. Focus all your awareness on this tightness and then think of something or someone you love and get that FEELING and then with that strong love feeling, keep your focus on that tight or even painful part of your neck. It also helps to again speak to that pain, which is just energy stuck there because of some past hurt or trauma programmed into your mind. Tell the pain it's o.k. to release from your body and dissolve. Speak out loud (if you can) lovingly as though it's a child trying to get your attention. It will leave happily. You see, you don't let go of it, like we have been told, IT LET'S GO OF YOU. I do this all the time. Once it's a habit and no one is around to commit you to a mental institution, you will see rapid results for yourself. Again, sounds crazy and I am in no way trying to convince you that this is what you should do. No shoulds. Only if you choose to and it resonates and you are curious to try it. Then, you will see for yourself if it works or not. Then you can trust yourself, not me, especially since I may be an alien.You can do this with bees, flies and even people. Remember hurt people, hurt people. Sending strong feelings and messages of love to someone who has hurt you will work in the same way the pain dissolved from your body. Just by feeling a strong intention of love and good will for the person who has hurt you, instantaneously relieves you of any pain, anger or sadness. If the person is in your presence and you can leave the situation saying that you love them and you need some space to take care of you now. And, you do just that. Loving and telling yourself whatever it is you have always wanted to hear from someone else , an adult or parents to tell you and they never did. Again, telling yourself from yourself is the only way our programmed brain will believe it. No one else can tell us, even if they do, we don't believe them until we have told ourselves over and over until we do believe it. At first it seems as though we are lying to ourselves, but like a husband or wife who has cheated and said they were sorry and then proved it by staying honest and true in their actions and you THEN trust and believe them again. The trouble is we have lied to ourselves so much and have treated ourselves so badly, that we ourselves, don't trust anything we say. That's why some time and effort and relearning how to treat and love ourselves is priority and takes time and focus

Another example of loving what is. If you are in a situation where you are being held captive or even at gunpoint, do the same thing. Either say something kind to the person or silently be aware in your mind's eye and project out radiant, strong feelings of love toward them. Remember, just like the crucifix in the old vampire movies, it really works. The famous author , Viktor E. Frankl, a holocaust survivor and wrote the book "Man's Search for Meaning". He tells about being in various concentration camps in Word War II and did this and more to survive the hell he was in. He swore they would never take over his mind and they never did. He didn't use the crucifix, of course, being Jewish, he did keep his mind on love and refused to let them take over his mind and cause him to fall in the depths of despair. The book is wonderful and a classic and well worth reading and shows how powerful we can be when we don't succumb to fear and being the victim. You always have the power to change your thoughts even in the extreme situation he was in. We may not be able to control what happens to us; although we can control our reaction to what happens and it starts with a thought that then turns into action.

Another example of this, I thought of the other day; in fact for some reason I've thought about this several times recently. I think they made a movie of it and I may not have all the details correct. Going from memory of something I either saw on the news or the person interviewed. I think it happened in Atlanta. This man broke into a single young woman's house or apartment. She was alone and I'm pretty sure he had a gun. She was definitely captive and somehow she remained calm and very kind to him. She started a conversation about Jesus and God and he turned himself in to police, left and became a devout Christian. The man himself was interviewed and told the story of how he came to turning himself in. As I said, I don't remember the details; it was a long time ago. It just always stayed in my mind and I use this story now to give another example of how love always wins.

Now you say, What if I'm going along with love in my heart and have forgiven everyone including myself and am feeling infused with joy and all at once someone drives by and shoots me dead?? What about that, huh? How did love win there? My explanation and belief, not saying it's true or I'm right, is just that it's your time. Exactly, precisely the time and way you were supposed to pass on. Love took you and love did win and so did you. And, since I believe, we really never die, our soul spirit is forever and ever. Has no beginning and no end. And, if you are in the state of joy and love when your body dies, it will just put you in a higher place and less to process and learn, your next time around. You may not believe in reincarnation and that is fine. I do believe after reading about and seeing people interviewed with Near Death Experiences (NDE). And the 1,000's of stories from therapists and past life regressions. Also, it's just that knowing within me that is very personal and feels true and makes sense. Which is what I am saying is important for your truth. You know by your feelings if something is true or not. If it's true for you, it feels light, if not it will feel heavy. Good compass when you are trying to make a decision. Now not only in spiritual teachings, there is more scientific research and proof of reincarnation. That is another reason to learn to love yourself more so you will be more loving, kind and generous to your neighbor because whatever you do to hurt yourself or another, you just have to come back and make it right with the same people. In reality, what you do to another you are doing to yourself. Again, you don't have to believe me or agree with me on reincarnation or anything that does not resonate with you. I'm just giving you information on what I have learned in my research and resources and may help you think about, question and contemplate. You will get your own answers to your own questions. As long as it's your question and not someone else's question or answer. I always ask for signs when I question something and want proof. I always get the sign. Yes or No. It takes practice and it is the best way to start learning to trust yourself instead of what you hear or read on social media and news; or from anywhere or anyone. Including me.

Einstein is a great example of someone who got all his answers from within. There were no books for him to go to. He had to come up with all his theories by asking and imagining. When I say, within, it's not just your own body/mind. It's still God/Source/Higher Power, Super Conscious; whatever you want to call it. It is that place within the quietness of your soul. That is why meditation is good for connecting with God/ Source and resolving, dissolving and creating whatever you desire. Even before meditation though, REMEMBER, Love/Accept What Is. You don't have to like it, just accept and then ask what now? What can I do ? Ask for help, whatever , just don't get stuck in the OMG why is this happening to me mode and the blame/shame cycle.

SPECIAL NOTE TO EMPATHS. For those of you who easily love and forgive and are constantly taking on others' pain and tend to be a doormat for others without your needs fulfilled or respected. Any situation or person that is causing you harm to this degree, go ahead and love and accept them or it, and then leave or say no more. Most importantly you spend time immediately, loving yourself more than ever before in order to dissolve and heal all the pain and transferred energy that is lingering within you and will eventually cause sickness and disease. After time and you are totally recharged, you may go back out again and even those people or situations won't be able to hurt you again, because you have built up your own immunity and trust yourself completely and know who to enter into partnerships with or not. People who are not empath tend to find it harder to accept and forgive and love another, as Empaths do naturally. This book is not intended for Empaths. There are several out there and I have read and have attended classes. If you are an empath, and want to learn more I recommend Anita Moorjani's new book "Sensitive is the New Strong "Anita is famous for her Near Death Experience and who Wayne Dyer discovered. I have also referenced her book that Wayne encouraged her to write called "Dying to be Me" about her near death experience. Reference at end of book.

Six
You Don't Have Like It

JUST BECAUSE IT is important to love/accept what is ,
doesn't mean you need to like it or even pretend to. Accepting
and forgiving and trying to be the saint and loving one when
underneath you are boiling with anger will never get you to
the heaven and bliss I am talking about. It will not be the way
to learn to love and trust yourself, for sure. Nor is the way to
argue, attack another especially if you've been holding in this
anger and hurt for a long time. Maybe, even a lifetime. When
we find ourselves depressed and or angry or especially fearful, we want to blame someone for it. Whatever comes up,
whether it is personal, political or spiritual, we tend to first

look for who/what to blame. And, that only makes things worse. I remember arguing with my X-husband who made it a career of being able to bring up whatever would push your buttons and argue the opposite of whatever your belief or opinion was. I would hear him argue a political point with one person one day and then argue the very next night with someone else taking the opposite view of the same issue he had argued the night before. I always said he should have been a great prosecuting attorney. In the ten years I was married to him, I never once won an argument. Because of the mental abuse I was experiencing and allowing, I thought I was sticking up for myself to argue back and even yell louder my defense. All it ever did was leave me exhausted and drained and he never saw my point of view. That is why you don't want to express your anger and blame to others regardless of how they receive it. It doesn't work. They don't change nor do they even hear you. However, take yourself out of the situation and use creative ways to express and dissolve your anger. Tell yourself it is o.k. to be angry and be supportive of yourself. Matt Kahn says that anger is an eruption of unexpressed passion and I agree with him. Using your creativity to express your anger is healing and works in dissolving the anger and pain. Some tools for the dissolution of anger are journaling all that you are feeling and how unfair it is and how you feel or blame another. Another way is to write a letter to the person or institution that you are so angry with and just let it all out in words you would never say out loud and to someone's face, just what you think of them. Hide the stamps and then just burn the letter after you are satisfied you have expressed yourself completely. Also, try painting a picture of the situation and emotion or, dance and sing it away. It will, I promise, transfer from your emotional body and return it back out to Source/God while speaking to yourself words of love and support. Over time, you just don't have any of those awful, anger, fearful feelings. They just disappear and you have more patience and understanding for those people who are experiencing their own pain and anger and don't know how to go about dissolving or getting any relief. You have to also be loving to yourself while letting your anger out in the writing and not feel guilty afterwards. That is what is keeping all the resentful feelings and anger inside you because you have somehow blamed yourself in some way and keep attracting these people and situations that trigger that hurt and pain that is stuck in your mind. Burn the letter then do the work to soothe yourself and heal the pain that you are feeling was caused by another.

A magical gift exercise for you You may do this before meeting with another person in person or on phone or in group meetings. Picture a rose of any color 12" in front of you. Everything in between your physical body and the rose is your's and only your space alone. Everything on the other side of the rose ,you give permission to the person or persons you are coming or in contact with. In your space you are giving yourself permission to have your own stories, your own beliefs and at the same time giving others the right to have their own space for their beliefs and stories.

What is so beautiful about this exercise is that any frustration, fear, whatever negative emotion you may have regarding this person or people, seems to lighten up or even disappear. You are protected and are not penetrating out negative emotions that others can read/and or feel coming from you. You can also use this for groups of people at meetings . Just set your rose up in front of you before the meeting and set a clear intention for the most benevolent outcome for yourself and all involved. After the meeting with the individual or group, mentally give them a rose as they walk away. They now have their own Permission rose to have the right to their own space. You may put more roses around you if you want and if you are out in a crowd. Put them 12", front, sides and back. Also, if your rose starts looking wilted then just replace it with another. I am in the habit now of seeing my rose first thing in the morning and it is already set up and will adjust around you as needed. You can always add a new or another rose before your meeting each day.

I learned all this from Jeffrey Allen from his Duality Course on MindValley. What I love about this besides it works miracles, is Jeffrey comes from a successful engineering background and is fact based and very reputable and authentic. When I, in the past, would go into energy healing exercises with family and friends, I got the impression they thought it was and I was far out and wooo woo and no one would pay any attention. I was coming from fear then and so I was projecting that on to them. However, now learning these techniques from scientific and fact based teachers, I have the confidence to share with others. Also, everything I do share, I have first tried myself and added the conflicts and learning problems that I had to overcome so I can help others experience the exercises more easily and freely. As I tell my clients, you don't have to do or believe anything I say, I could be wrong and have been several times. I'm just offering things I've experienced and worked wonders for me. For example, the rose exercise seems far out especially if you don't understand how energy works which Jeff does and explains so well in his course. When you actually try it for yourself and experience the results, you don't have to really understand how or why it works; you just feel very powerful and at peace because it does.

I'm seeing myself as the Angie Referral Service for methods, ideas, techniques, and findings of other people, that totally blow your mind and bring you peace at the same time. Although, there are always new findings coming up and new classes for me to take. So, what I may have taught or shared last year may be entirely different this year. I have noticed that what I believed to be true, I find out isn't anymore. Speaking of Jeffrey, he told the story of his Physics teacher telling everyone at the beginning of his class that everything he is about to teach is not true and not to believe him. Although, it is the best they know now. That is why or one of the reasons why, I love the adventure I am on and all the new information coming up in science, the universe and human nature and consciousness. There is no end to the vast knowledge we can attain by just being open minded and then choosing what feels right for you and also letting others do the same. Just like the rose. We will not only heal ourselves and dissipate our fear; we will also do the same for others by just allowing and loving.

Seven
The New Earth

YEARS AGO ECKHART Tolle wrote a book entitled The New Earth and he and Oprah did a computer Training Class; not sure if it was zoom back then, but similar to zoom. I read the book and took class with Oprah and Eckhart. I don't remember all the details of the book or class, although I've now read all of Eckhart's books and practiced his teaching all the time. Mainly Stay PRESENT. What I am wondering now is if and I'm sure I could find out from one of his YouTube talks or courses online, if he was predicting the new earth that is coming into form now. This version I'm talking about now hasn't been proven in mainstream science and is more in the area of the part of the society that doesn't want us to know and who are trying so hard to separate us and create fear. I'm just learning about what is taking place with the earth which is just as much alive and part of God/Source. I came across on YouTube Delores Cannon, who was a past life regression therapist and under hypnosis these people would go back into past lives and then one day someone went back to a past planet. After that there were 1,000's more, while they were under a trance, she would ask questions which in the beginning were questions the client had. Then, some other voice came in which she recorded that she would refer to as their subconscious, which turned out to be not just one person's subconscious but an universal one. Whatever, it was they knew things and would explain in detail things that the person Doris was working with had no way of knowing. They said that there was a Confederate of Stars that was very interested and wanted to help the earth and the beings on earth. They are bound by the law of free will from the number 1 Creator of all, and cannot interfere with our free will even if we are on the road to self destruction of our entire species. They compared earth/us to Atlantis where they had developed into the magnificent planet with extraordinary high tech way ahead of what we have now. Unfortunately, some Scientists were experimenting with things that would be harmful and could destroy their planet, which they did. With us it all started after the atomic bomb, that the Star Beings decided they had to get involved somehow or we could not only blow up our planet but also the whole hemisphere around us. So, they came up with this plan that they would ask for volunteers to come down on earth and many who have never had a past life on earth without Karma, in order to help all the earth beings move to the 5th Dimension and new earth which is only peace and love. There were three waves of volunteers starting in the 1940's. These volunteers are called Star Seeds, Wanderers, LightWorkers and the children now are referred to as Indigos, which are the most brilliant of all. It is all done by them being light beings, sending light and love telepathically to all beings, all catastrophes, all pandemics, anything that is harmful or negative; in order to move with the earth. Keep your thoughts filled with love for yourself and others. It's even more important to learn to love yourself FIRST, because when you truly are loving yourself, you automatically love everything outside of you and everything outside of you starts changing into love and beauty. It is because we have collectively been walking around drugged, depressed, angry, fearful and full of hate that the world looks like it does. We create our own life and world by our thoughts and feelings. It's important though that those that are sending love and light to help transcend the collective, also honor their own pain and trauma first and not try to stay positive all the time without first dealing with and releasing their own pain, trauma and fear. Again, it always starts with us first. If you are constantly angry and resentful and especially fearful then expect whatever you are angry or fearful about to present itself right in your space. Unless however, you put your Permission rose there for yourself and others.

Eight
Back to The Future

MAY I BE the first to congratulate you for the open mind you have if you are still with me after all I've shared. Doesn't matter if you agree, believe or think I am crazy, you have one of the first traits of genius which is curiosity. I don't know if that is really one of the first traits. I do know however it is an important one and kept Einstein and other geniuses going even after massive so-called failures So, since you are still with me especially after the last chapter, then thank you and congratulations. I've never shared that part with anyone and you are the first and you are still with me. Back to earth now and our everyday stuff going on. See, I told you I loved you and I just feel I can trust you regardless if you agree with me.

I listened to Bill O'Reilly's podcast today. I haven't listened to him since I first found his podcast a year ago. What I found interesting was as usual he is reporting the recent events and about the investigation going on regarding the January 6, 2021 attack on the White House. I had heard the findings or part of them on my local channel 10 news, however, as usual he brought up some good points. It's crazy how even though the police and different areas of government were warned that it was going to happen and many would have guns ; they were not at all prepared. O'Reilly believes that focus should stay on the absurd and outrageous behavior of those involved with the attack. They have arrested 400+ people involved with the violence and the FBI will be offering deals to these people in order to find out more information. Where did they come from: Who/what was behind the attack, etc. Instead or possibly he said , the Democratic Party may just use this as a way to blow up Trump and all the focus goes to that instead of getting to the root cause of the issue. Although, I don't like blaming the Democrats or other individuals which it's not them, it's the power behind them that is a low energy group trying to control and separate us. It's that kind of thing that goes on all the time. I do believe we should focus on those questions O,Reilly said on Where and Who, What. The power behind all of this is only wanting to keep our focus off finding who is behind anything because it's them. Just keep blaming it on the democrats or the republicans or anyone so we will keep divided and fight and blame each other. Again, it really comes down to what station you watch and listen to that determines who and what to fear. The real negative force behind this all is really speaking through all media and like my husband did by switching sides depending on who he was arguing with. The media/ whatever the vehicle, is convincing you of the wrongness, evil in the other person, party, organization, country and then convinces you what is wrong with and who is behind it and how hateful and evil the democrats are and what they all believe. Then the same group/ is behind the media and whatever then is trying to convince us how hateful and evil the Republicans are. These powerful Double Agents, but small groups own the media and much more and are not interested in making more money. They have more than enough. They are only interested in worldwide power and control. And they are getting it through mind control, through the media and government that they are behind and control. O'Reilly also brought up on his podcast that he was disappointed in OBama, who I love, in a recent CNN interview which OBama said, I don't have an exact quote, however, something like the media on the right promotes the faults and actions of the black community and history, which O'Reilly said was true and agreed with him. What he was disappointed in though was OBama didn't say that the left did the same thing in regard to white population. He said, OBama could have turned to the CNN interviewer and said you do the same thing, but he didn't. That was what disappointed O'Reilly. That is exactly what I am saying in this book. I don't know if O'Reilly was making the point for his party or if he knows, as I am aware, that the media is really not to be trusted and are using mind control methods to keep us divided. I also liked the way O'Reilly used the word disappointed in OBama for not saying both sides do it, instead of tearing him down verbally in hateful words as others do on the mainstream news stations. I believe it is ok and necessary to tear down the system, processes or event which is harmful or not working or whatever you are against; I do not agree under any consequences to tear down the person and that seems to be the norm in past 20 years at least, and keeps us from focusing on and stopping the system behind the whole thing. Before we leave earth and politics, I want to say something regarding Trump. I did not vote for him and I honestly did not see him as being the caliber of person that I believe would be best in representing America as the President of the United States. I did, however, practice what I preached and did not rebel, blame, hate or fear him. I would send light around him to get the insight and guidance to make the best decisions for the highest good of us all and the world. I also heard him say several times that the election was rigged and getting all his supporters riled up. I thought to myself that the election has probably been rigged for more than 20 years and that's how he got in. Just my belief and there is data out there that does question and after doing some research and just going by my own intuition and gut, there probably is truth to the elections being rigged. Again, don't believe me especially since it's just a gut feeling

I have after I've heard it from others. It's not the democrats or republicans doing it though, if it is happening and by now you know who is behind it, instead of blaming a party. I also believe the majority of those people who vandalized and attacked on January 6, 2021, were not Trump support-ers. Just like all those people who vandalized and destroyed during the Black Lives Matter marches. They were plants originating from this small but powerful force that is trying to divide us and take control. And, I'm not telling you this to frighten you. I am telling you this so you can be aware and do your own research and ask your own questions and find your own truth. I am above all telling you this to wake you up to the fact the enemy is not the blacks, or police, or white supremists, or muslims, or the chinese or the russians or the liberals or conservatives and what you can do to win and stop the real enemy and above all without fear. That is what they feed off of, FEAR. We can win with love, which they cannot exist in, like the crucifix..

Again, don't believe me. I'm just the messenger who came to this planet loaded with all the things necessary to aid in the transcendence and ascension to the next dimension for all those who are ready and have raised their vibration to be LOVE just 51% of the time. I always feel bad about those who won't make it and want to stay in the negativity. I've been told that I will mess up my own transition as well as many others if I focus on that group. They will eventual-ly move up, Everyone is on their own path and have their own learning and experiences to follow. Just keep focused on your own path and the changes you want to make within yourself that makes you happy, healthy and wise.

Before I leave the subject of Bill O'Reilly, I have had a vision for years that Bill O'Reilly and Marianne Williamson would be on my podcast someday and have a political discussion. This was even before Marianne ran for President. I think that would be a great conversation to listen to. Even though Marianne is my spiritual teacher and mentor, I have learned more about politics and fact based history from her than anyone else. In fact, it was Marianne who woke us up in the spiritual realm to be aware and involved politically. Like myself, many in the Spiritual community would be non-political and totally uninvolved. That, she said, was one of the reasons we found ourselves where we are today. All the negativity and corruption got in while we were uninvolved. And, for me, my head was in the clouds. Like the food industry. How did all that happen and why? Arsenic in baby food, chemicals causing obesity in our food, bleach in our flour and what's with paying our farmers NOT to grow food. I can't believe I wasn't aware of any of that until it was common practice. I still don't understand or know what's behind it all and it wasn't until 8-10 years ago I read a book about eating/ buying local food and what is in season and all the food coming in from all over the world and what that takes to do it. I then made it a point to learn more. Being aware and bringing all the information to the forefront has changed our food world immensely. At first, it was hard to find organic in the grocery stores and when you did it was very expensive. Now, it is so much more affordable and the big grocery chains have their own organic line and it is very affordable. I always read labels now and I never did before. I became involved and aware of what was going on. I love to go to farmers markets and living in Ohio, I only wish we could go back to having farms fully producing and we get our food from our local grocery fresh from the farms; not from Chile, for God sakes. I know dream on, I just love the small town atmosphere. I loved going to the market and getting your fresh food daily. I remember seeing ladies 75-80 years old , in Italy, pulling their daily market food in their cart, walking up a cobblestone street. Love it!!!

So, I took Marianne's coaching and got involved with politics as I did with what's going on with my food, and one thing led to another and politics became the entryway to an enormous opening into a vast world filled with infinite possibilities and how to create and choose the life you want. Remember your thoughts and feelings create your reality and world. So, let's all come together and create a beautiful, plentiful, peaceful and above all loving world together. We can start with our own selves, then, city, state, country and then world and then go to the moon.

Nine
What About Alzheimer's

WHAT IF ALZHEIMER'S also didn't have to happen to us just because we are aging? What if that too is only what you believe and we could reverse any symptoms of that also. Those tests we have to take each year in our doctor's office to see if we are falling into Alzheimer's is ridiculous. Being 78 at this writing and along with everyone I know that is on Medicare; we are all equally discouraged regarding the mandated verbal tests that our doctors are mandated to do each year at our annual appointment. I and many others dread these questions and test whether we are still competent based on a list of memory questions. When we were in our

30's and 40's or even before, we forgot things a lot. I did so much that it just became a joke with me and others. I was not threatened at all. I had so much new information coming in that I could not remember stuff that I did not need anymore. It's not that Alzheimer's doesn't exist and many are suffering from it. I do believe that the fear being put out there about it though has caused many, out of constant fear of getting it, can cause the nervous system to send messages of fear to the brain and create a pathway or some trigger that can cause the Altziemers. Bruce Lipton, Ph.D. has proven in his research that 5% of our health, money making abilities come from genes. 95% come from our belief systems, stories and environment. I have put a reference to one of his CD sets with Dr. Joe Dispenza at the end of this book so you can learn more about him and his findings if you are interested. Also, just google or look on YouTube for him, there is plenty to prove his findings for the skeptic and again opening your mind and then deciding on your own what resonates with you and take it or leave it. Remember, what you believe and feel can create your reality and Dr. Lipton does a great job at helping to explain this. And, don't worry. Just a few fearful thoughts or even several will manifest and or make you sick. It is genuine focus, fear and intense feeling on a long term basis that can and will create exactly what you want or not want. So, before I go to the doctor and take that test, I start saying to myself how I love the test and how well I do on the test and have stopped telling myself how much I hate the damn thing. I told my doctor this time how much I dreaded taking the test and how I was scared to death in the past of failing and then maybe they would commit me. I told the nurse this AFTER I had passed with flying colors. I love my Doctor and he and his nurse apologize for these tests and I realize they have to do it because it is required by Medicare. I wonder why?? I have a friend who has had two MRI's and was put on medication, who is scared to death about taking tests and afraid she has or is getting Alzheimer's . She is absolutely fine and one of the most alert, strong women I know. She is 80 and looks 60 and I told her one day at lunch everything I have written here to convince her to convince herself that she is just fine and is not losing her mind. I think a lot of the symptoms of Alzheimer's are really just NOT BEING PRESENT. I've put things in the refrigerator that belonged in the cupboard or crazy things, leaving my water bottle somewhere I couldn't find and then it's in some weird place. Forgetting someone's name I have known for years. I used to remember everyone's name, years ago when I was a secretary. It was my job then to remember names for my boss who didn't. It's not my job now to remember names and as I said at the beginning when I was younger, I am bringing so much new information in now that some of the old memories are not needed. It may also be that some people who are living in the past or afraid of the future, stop remembering because they do not want to remember especially if there is trauma and pain that has not been dealt with. And, frankly as I explained earlier, we are all holding on to some kind of trauma either huge or even as simple as one of your parents being late picking you up from school one day and then instantly we form a decision in our mind why and what we will do to protect ourselves from it happening again. Then because we didn't really see the real reason and never were equipped to deal with what happened as a child we then get triggered by any similar situation that happens in our life and blame the person or situation for what happened and get retraumatized all over again. And, we do it over and over. No wonder everyone is blaming everyone else. It's worse now than ever before and if we just realized we have to find those traumas' within us and release and care for ourselves and not blame the other because they are only appearing in our lives because we are attracting them. We would not have any more conflict with another if we just identified and released our own stuff. Another expert in this field is Jennifer McClean and her Spontaneous Transformation Technique which she has classes on and also a book of the same name that I refer to at the end of book. I've taken her course too and used it with my Clients and it is amazingly helpful. It seems as though we are getting off the subject of Alzheimer's, however, my intention is to always guide you from fear to other material and solutions.

I remember years ago we used to laugh about looking up symptoms and diseases in a medical journal, before the internet, and would end up believing we had everything we read about. I believe that is what is happening now with Alzheimer's with all the media and talk and fear about it, we start believing ourselves that we are getting it. I have a male friend that says at least once a week that he is probably getting it and that his memory is so bad. He has the most incredible memory of anyone I know. He is a musician and remembers the words to every song he sings, which are 100's starting back from the 1940's to 1980's and still learns new and recent songs. Really, the man is brilliant, gifted and has the charisma of Cary Grant (even looks) as far as I'm concerned but he is talking himself into the belief that he is falling apart in his old age. Not true, but if he believes it then it will surely happen. I wonder if we can refuse to take that test each year. Especially if they are using that to determine early signs of memory loss. If I had not used my mind control to get myself all alert and ready for the test, I most likely would have failed because I was so nervous about taking it. There are many like me. Does anyone know why Medicare requires the doctors to do these tests? I'll bet Dr. Oz knows and would tell us the truth.

So my dear readers and the GREATEST senior citizen generation ever and who have lived much longer than THEY expected and are looking better than ever. Just relax and know you will know what you need to know and refuse to take that damn memory test. It is stupid and doesn't proof anything except it has been able to stress us out enough that we may not answer the questions correctly. Keep talking to yourself in the mirror and saying, I remember what I need to and/or my memory is just fine. It works perfectly for me. You may want to do it silently if you don't live alone so as not to be committed!!

And, by all means in any sickness or physical or mental pain, see your doctor. Do the procedures called for. Sometimes we need the extra help when we especially do not feel the faith and strength to let go and let God. God/Source is always in the Doctor and medicine too.

Ten

Surprise Bonus; How to Manifest What You Want in Your Life

IF I WOULD have named this book anything with the word manifest in it, I probably would right off the bat, sell 100's or even 1,000's of copies. Everyone is writing and selling books on manifesting and the law of attraction. Although I do want to sell my book, more than just selling it, I want it to come into the hands of those who are meant to and are ready to hear and experience this information and be part of the world wide transformation that is happening. And, I want nothing more than to bring this information to you all so that you can live a life no matter what your age, more inspired and extraordinary than you could ever imagine. If you were not supposed to read this book, you would not be reading or listening to it now. I believe that for myself and that we are always guided to what we need to learn or experience and it always comes at the right time. Like the saying goes, the teacher will come when the student is ready. I'm putting in new information on manifesting because it is real and true and since you now have read all the more important information, I have already shared. (Unless ofcourse you cheated and jumped to this chapter, which is fine but you will miss the real formula). The previous information really is more important than just manifesting everything you want because if you don't know how to clear out all those old fears and learn how to get back in control of your mind from the media, society and those out to control it for you, it won't matter if you manifest all your dreams and get all those things you want. Somehow, those old beliefs that you didn't even remember you had, will pop up and sabotage everything you have manifested that you thought would be what you wanted i.e.; to be loved, secure and safe and acknowledged. I remember my mother telling me, be careful what you pray for, you just may get it. Good advice. Although, I really wasn't sure what she meant at the time. As a child most of what I prayed for I did receive. As an adult and early on as a single parent, I was praying and setting goals which I would write down and would get everything I prayed for or intended until I didn't. It seemed to not work for me when I was trying the hardest. Doing all the steps, visualizing, writing down affirmation like crazy and repeating them over and over. What started it NOT happening for me was in my relationships and my health. Starting with my health. I thought just declaring my wellness, perfect health, meditating, praying ,western meds and doctors and acupuncture and taking responsibility for something I had done that attracted whatever health issue I had, would heal me. Even demanding the healing, which I did, the last time I was sick. What I am intending to do in this chapter on manifestation is give you the tools in each area of your lives that most of us want to manifest good in. I am also going to give you the most up to date effective processes which although in the beginning some and many were not effective, it was a beginning. Again, the people like me who were interested in these new techniques, especially alternative health techniques, were ridiculed supposedly from the Medical Field. Why would they ridicule people and Health Practitioners, who used turmeric instead of steroids and other alternatives like whole foods, plant based diets, meditation, etc to heal chronic illnesses? Especially condemn them and in some cases Medical Doctors using or associating with alternative health products, processes in some cases lost their licenses. This is just another question to wonder about and ask yourself. It's obvious to me. I also 100% agree to use these alternatives ALONG with seeing your doctor. It is important you do not just stop taking your meds and/or refuse to go to a doctor because you believe you can heal yourself. In fact you really aren't healing yourself. Your body is healing itself. That is the part I had to learn the hard way. I had to learn to be present with my pain and/or illness and give it the focus and attention as I did with my feelings as a child wanting your attention. You have probably heard that your body talks to you and lets you know something is going wrong. It usually starts giving you signs before the actual problem manifests. Again, pay attention to yourself, ask what your body is trying to tell you. Maybe slow down, watch what you are eating. Whether you are feeling a small irritation or are experiencing chronic severe pain or illness; it works the same for healing. Go in your mind and to that place in your body that you are feeling the discomfort and focus directly with the feeling of love. Just keep your attention on the point the pain or discomfort resides in. The mistake we, or I made, was I was frantically trying to get rid of it. Whatever it is. I remember saying, I wanted the 24 hour flu over in 12 hours. I joked about that in my younger years, but really meant it. Keep thinking it's like your other feelings that pop up, It is wanting your attention and love. And, as you experience and stay with your pain or illness, keep breathing deeply in and out. With every breath out, you feel relief and emptiness until gradually it all subsides. Practice this on small things like headaches and cramps in your legs. At first you feel the pain very strongly, then it seems to just move out of your body as you continue to focus all your attention and feelings of love on it. It is just energy that is stuck again. This energy is in your body. Your trauma and emotional pain energy is in your mind. We are all just energy. This is real.

This is just one small, but very effective exercise that I have experienced myself. For the big stuff and overall, I think the very best technique and training in healing your body, no matter what or how bad it is, is Brandy Gillmore's training. Check out her podcast and link to her website www. BrandyGilmore.com and her podcast Heal Yourself. Change Your Life.

I won't go into her story here. You can find out for yourself if you like, by going on to her website and/or the above link. After hearing her story, and listening to her podcast, I bought her three week class which was and is extraordinary. I've been studying this with many teachers for years and Brandy's techniques, which she created herself, are the most effective of anything I have learned before. She also proves to you through her class and exercises that not only does your body heal permanently also your life changes and expands greater than you have ever thought possible. Because as she teaches and you get it , your thoughts and your feelings create your life. I bought the program not because I had any physical problems, which I didn't and still don't. I bought the program because she is living proof it works and she explains that not only do you heal your ailment but totally change your life. She had been confined to bed for seven years in terrible chronic pain. She could hardly walk and was in a wheelchair and every part of her was a mess after a tragic accident. She more than recovered and I won't spoil her story. If you are curious, just check her out on above link and podcast

Manifesting in Relationships: This is another sought after desire and 1000's of books to show you how. In fact, I worked and tried so hard on this one, that it literally made me sick. Really sick. Let's just say, I didn't do any of the things I wrote about at the beginning of this book. I was obsessed and completely determined to MAKE my relationship work INSTEAD of letting them be and responding accordingly and always coming back to myself when I found myself triggered or in conflict. The #1 reason for me that I wasn't manifesting what I wanted in my relationships is because I wasn't loving and trusting myself. For me, which may not be the same for all, I believed everyone else's needs were more important than my own. In fact, somewhere in my mind from some prior childhood experience, I had to be the one to make everyone else happy. It wasn't necessary for them to fulfill any of my needs. Instead if I did have one, it appeared that would be the one thing others would not give me. I thought since I was already a happy person and I didn't believe that anyone else can make you happy, I would just give all my total joy, love, peace and sacrifice without any need or belief any chance of receiving back from those I loved. The one exception to that was from my grandchildren. The joy, love and peace I felt from each one of them actually contributed to my owning my own perfect and free self expression now. It felt like an influx of love transmission whenever I was with them.

Now here is another tried and true exercise I finally did and it is working. I've gone back to every relationship which

I have experienced pain or regret and healed that part of myself that was hurt. NO matter what the other person did or didn't do, I did not spend any time on blaming them. All the focus was on me and where I hurt and most of all accepting and acknowledging myself of what all I had been through. Telling myself no wonder I was so hurt and it wasn't my fault that I had forgotten to take care of myself and just gave everything away until I was empty; and then everyone around me felt the emptiness cause I wasn't expanding out that love that is me anymore. Just like you can't love anyone until you love yourself. I was pouring out to others who didn't love themselves and were believing they could only get love from another, till I was exhausted and emptied myself. Like anything, you have to make deposits into your account, if you want to keep writing checks. And, in this case, deposits in your heart, in order to keep it all working for you.

YOU don't have to know why you are hurting or why the relationship is not working. All you need to do is stop the bleeding, stop the pain. And,the only and quickest and lasting way to do this is for YOU,YOURSELF ALONE, to go inside and love that part of you that is hurting as you would a newborn. Remember, when you fell and had a boo boo and your mommy kissed it and said it's all right now and it was. Even if you never had that experience, now you are the parent and do it for yourself. I just heard recently that a study by some reputable organization or research center, I think it was Heart Math, actually said through some trial tests, that the #1 most rapid way to healing was kissing the hurt. Sometimes it would be instantly and the cut would heal. The point is to go back to you and your body, heart and soul who is crying out for YOUR love and kiss. Kiss your hand right now and put it on your cheek and say I love you and I am never going to leave you. Watch how you feel in that instant.

Another wonderful practice which I am in the process of being a certified practitioner, and that will give you an easy and rapid loving transmission is HO'OPONOPONO. Without going into all the background of what this is and why it works, I am going to give you the words to say to yourself over and over as you are healing and learning to love yourself. This is really good when you have been triggered. There are extraordinary facts and in-depth teaching which if you would like to learn what, why and how regarding Ho'oponopono. I believe the best training and delivery is with Joe Vitali and Dr. Hulinn. There are online trainings and Joe Vitali has written a book called Zero Limits. Excellent book and very informative. I'm taking the certification program with him and Dr. Hulinn. This is the little verse that heals everything. Always say it for yourself. Never use it to try to fix another. It's a prayer and has to be focused on yourself even if you are upset, worried about another. As always, first we heal ourselves. Here is the prayer. I LOVE YOU. I'M SORRY. PLEASE FORGIVE ME. THANK YOU.

That's it folks and it would be best if you held yourself in your hands, self hug until you feel safe. and/or place your hand on your heart while you are saying it. It especially works well if you are having trouble sleeping because of stuff going through your mind. Just say it over and over till you drift off to a healing, deep sleep. I promise it works!!!

NOW LETS MANIFEST A NEW RELATIONSHIP, PARTNER/SOULMATE AND/OR JAQUAR IN YOUR GARAGE.

As I mentioned earlier, manifestation, especially for stuff we want, is in great demand right now. I've been studying all these things starting in the 60's, which has grown immensely. It used to be the self help, spiritual, health/wellness books were in a small corner of the bookstore. Now it is the entire floor of a bookstore. Before I give you the easiest, best proven way to manifest whatever you want, I want to say again until you spend time healing, loving yourself and communicating directly with God/Universe, it won't matter how much you manifest in $$, relationships, body shape, cars, houses, fame, power, academia, or whatever you think you need or desire. It will never be enough and the joy and peace of mind that you will realize and experience by knowing and loving yourself first, will not be present in your greatest accomplishment, achievement or relationship. Also, what you desire no matter what it is, what you truly want is the emotion that you think it will give you. That is why you have to practice FEELING those emotions you are trying to get from the outside world, within yourself first. NOW here it is; easy peasy and by all means make sure you really want what you say you want, cause you WILL get it. It doesn't work just part of the time or even most of the time, it works all of the time. The only reason it will not work, is if you change your mind, or doubt you will get it or if you think you don't deserve it.

1. Write down something you would really love to have. It may be best for the first time, to pick something small then when you see how great it worked, go for the gusto.

2. BIG FAT TIP: LEAVE OPEN THE PERSON WHEN YOU ARE WANTING TO MANIFEST A ROMANTIC RELATIONSHIP. I WAS TOLD THIS SEVERAL TIMES AND DIDN'T LISTEN AND WOULD WRITE IN THE SPECIFIC PERSON'S NAME FOR MY PARTNER OR ROMANTIC LOVE RELATIONSHIP — WRONG. Leave it open with the wording for example a man or woman who cherishes me or whatever you want from the relationship , just no specific names.

3. Envision whatever you wrote down taking place as you desired. For example, receiving flowers from a loved one. Now see in your vision, in your imagination,and if you can't see, just do the best you can with emphasis on the FEELING. On the flower receiving example, see yourself doing nothing , sitting on the sofa and maybe feeling ok but a little bored or lonely or whatever you are feeling in the now. Then notice in your imagination, doorbell rings, perk up, get up to go to the door. See yourself opening the door and wondering who it is. Then you see a delivery person holding two dozen white and red roses. He hands them to you and walks

away. You are so excited, FEEL it as you picture yourself holding roses. Then look at the card and be elated. See yourself and especially FEEL yourself. Then either end there or put roses in a vase that you already had ready to receive the flowers.

4. Now, very important and probably most important next to the feeling part is to LET IT GO. Do not tell anyone. Don't do anything to help make it happen and most of all do not for one second, doubt or think it won't happen. If you start thinking its stupid or doubting it will stop the whole process. You will have to start all over in Step 1. Because, it's your thoughts and feelings that are creating your life and outcome; so, when you change your mind, then your outcome changes. An analogy that is used a lot is like planting seeds in a garden. We plant the flower seeds and expect the flower. We plant the bean seeds and expect beans. We do not keep going out and digging it up to see if they are growing. We also don't get flowers where we planted beans and vice versa. We only expect and probably even envision the flowers wherever they were planted and the beans to appear where they were planted. The envisioning and sticking with it, is vital in your desire manifesting. Just do the vision of the end result of whatever you are wanting to manifest. Stay tuned into that every time any doubt comes up and above all do not try to figure it out , or how it's going to happen or what you can do. If you need to do something, it will come to you. Like

a phone call from the delivery service asking for your address for the flowers as in the example above, then you can do something, give them the address. Or, you may just get an intuitive message to go somewhere or make a call and you have no idea why. Just keep listening to your inspiration.

5. That's it! Just go along with whatever comes up in your life and enjoy and be grateful for the actual manifestation when it appears. And be sure and say not only THANK YOU, AND also KEEP IT COMING. No glass ceilings here. That is another mistake most make, is thinking its once in a lifetime occurrence and that's it, so GUESS WHAT, it is. So be sure and add Keep It Coming to your Thank You. It will be impossible for it not to manifest unless you have doubted or changed your mind or the vision in any way. Also, it will not work if you are wanting to harm yourself or another. Please email me at SallyPreston@DreamBuilderCoach. com any manifestation you would like to share. I love it when everything works out for you!!!

Eleven
Self Care Extraordinaire

REST IS PRIOR TO MOTION AND STILLNESS PRIOR TO ACTION
TAOIST PHILOSOPHY

WE HAVE BEEN taught and literally programmed into us the more we do, the more we sacrifice, the more we put into work, family, home, community and so on, the more valuable we are. We have learned the belief system that our self worth is defined by what we DO and how much we give, rather than who we are. Hopefully, you are now ready to choose what to think and believe and want more than anything else to be who YOU ARE and live the rest of your life loving and choosing what you do, what you believe, who you want to be with, and always envisioning the love, beauty and goodness in this world and stare down anything to the contrary, using the light and love and power inside of you to melt down and evaporate the darkness , just like the wicked witch in the Wizard of Oz. So, you can do all this if you find time to just rest your beautiful body and soul and care for yourself more deeply than ever before and just send out all these wonderful thoughts of love and envisioning how you want your world to be. The more rested, relaxed and filled with feelings of love you are, the faster you see the changes around you.

Here is a link to the most extraordinary ,sometimes instant healing technique of the century. It's called EFT or Tapping. I've included a link to how to do the tapping and examples of what to say while tapping on the meridians. Tapping targets the root cause of health and wellness challenges by inter-rupting the body's stress response quickly and effectively. Tapping is a powerful tool for enabling health on multiple levels: mental, emotional, and physical. From depression, anxiety, and stress related disorders like PTSD and fibromy-algia to physical pain and a lot more. When combined with a healthy lifestyle, including a wholesome plant rich diet, reg-ular physical exercise, and natural supplements to support health at a systematic level, tapping is a fast acting, non inva-sive way to proactively manage the stress that so often leaves our bodies vulnerable to disease. To get the whole scoop and statistical and proven medical and life changing examples with scientific research and proof check out Nick Ortner online on YouTube How to use EFT Tapping with Nick Ortner and his book The Tapping Solution and the Movie with the same name. There is also a Tapping App. This truly does, in some cases, work instantly. It is easy and quick. For the overall thorough change though to your body, mind and entire Life, I still strongly recommend Brandy Gilmore.

Now my dear ones. You are all set. You have enough tools now to live the life of your dreams, look and feel 20 to 30 years younger and literally start living the best years of your life. If you follow through on this wellness path and expand your consciousness and practice and use as many of the tools I have given you in this book, IT JUST HAPPENS. . You wake up one morning and you have this wonderful feeling, everything looks bright and filled with color and light, all these great people and experiences start coming into your life and view and you can't wait to see what the day will bring. Then, you know, you've made it and created it. Heaven on earth and the New Earth. Or, maybe you really don't want that right now and are comfortable just doing what you've been doing, then that's fine too, no change, your choice.

Twelve

Acceptance Rather than Judgment. Shot or No Shot.

WHEN I FIRST started writing this book it was right after the vaccinations for COVID came out and everything was opening up again and we didn't have to wear masks anymore and there was such joy and feeling of freedom. I know for me there was. I was happy wearing a mask even in restaurants at the time because we could take them off when we ate and because I wasn't afraid of getting the virus myself and if I did, I would not be holding anyone else responsible for me getting sick. Most of us felt protected because we had the vaccine. We were feeling completely safe and no worries. It was great. My family could come to see me again once they were vaccinated and were sure they would not carry the virus to me. I felt great and protected and made a long flight trip to California with a layover in Denver that was supposed to be three hours that ended up to be seven hours. The plane I was supposed to take out of Denver kept moving the departure time which we found out later was due to mechanical problems. When my plane finally did arrive it was a brand new one which was great, cause who wants to get on a plane that has been detained because of mechanical problems? I used my acceptance technique while waiting for the plane and knew everything would work out for me and not let the situation take control of my mind and cause me to feel frustrated, angry or fearful. I kept listening to uplifting music, being grateful for all the places I could walk around and look at in the airport, especially after being isolated for a year in my home. I was so happy just thinking of seeing my daughter, son in law, my three grandchildren and two great grandchildren who would be waiting for me to arrive in California.

When something happens you do not have control over and there isn't anything you can do to change it in the moment, then your FREE CHOICE is to accept and concentrate on whatever will bring you feelings of joy, love and peace. Or, you can start judging the situation or person and let that turn into anger, blame, shame and/or anxiety. It's still your choice. Choose to keep your power and not just give it away by choosing to judge instead of accepting the situation and still keep your power to control what your mind is creating. Although, if you are feeling hurt or fear because of anyone else or anything else , then first feel it and acknowledge it and soothe yourself and accept and love and tell yourself comforting things that you wished you would have heard from your parents and or others as a child. Then choose to choose again and concentrate on the things that bring you joy as I explained above. And, above all don't blame or beat up on yourself because you did judge, blame or get angry. Just know it is important now to love yourself more. AND BREATHE. It will instantly put you in the present moment and also lowers your blood pressure if you tend to have that problem during stress or upset. I have a breathing exercise on YouTube that you may check out if you need or want to.

As of this writing now, August 2021, things are changing back again to masks and rising in COVID because of the Delta variance. What the media and doctors are telling us is that this is worse than the original virus and the hospitals are over crowding again. Businesses are again requiring masks and in addition to that many (all in San Francisco) are requiring that you have proof of vaccination. In the beginning when they were first opening up restaurants and other businesses, we were told those not vaccinated should wear a mask and there was no proof of vaccination needed. I believe that we should have and utilize our God given free choice to decide what will go and not go into our bodies. I know that I have not been very complimentary of the BIG

PHARMA INDUSTRY previously in this book and it may come across as judging more than accepting. I remember at the very beginning of COVID saying to myself and others, now watch Big Pharma come up with a vaccine and become the big heroes. When in the previous few years or so we were cracking down on opioids and it was also being made known publicly how some antidepressants were making people worse, not better and many deaths and suicides. Doctors stopped freely re-prescribing opioids and it became much harder instead of in the past, easy to get the pills which has caused the massive addiction in this country.My bet is that all that bad publicity and the restrictive parameters in the hospitals and doctors' offices had around these drugs, caused the stock of some of these drug companies to drop. I looked at the history for one of them and saw a graph showing early years up to 1990 just flat and shares around $5.00. Then 1990, started upward going up as high as $25 in the year 2000. Then started going down as low as $7 or $8. And, then 2010-2020 very gradually started climbing with the highest boost in 2020 to $40. and today August, 2021 $48-$50. So, for me and I may be wrong and I'm no wall street stock expert, it does look like they did become the heroes and also made them lots of money with the COVID vaccine. This is not a judgment. It is an observation. Back when I thought they would become hero's with the vaccine and take the negative press off of them, I also said to myself; oh well, I hope they do come up with a vaccine so that will relieve the terrible fear that is spreading. And, since fear is a magnate and it is attracting the COVID more fiercely than ever, it will stop the fear and slow down the spread. And, I believe it did. Just like the placebo is just as effective or in some cases more than the real shot or pill, it's our mind that does the healing and in this case dissipated the fear and everyone was so happy. Also many of us prayed for a cure and/or miracle for COVID and the vaccination could be just that.

What I do believe is we are entitled to choice and what we individually feel is right for our body. That no-one has the right to demand you do something you don't want to do. It's the same thing with a mask, no mask. It turned into a political battle of right or wrong and what station you listen to in order to find out what is right or wrong. It is the SYSTEMS behind all this that are wanting to stay in control and are only able to do that if they divide us. That's what they try to do with all the issues out there now is put the blame on anyone or anything to keep the attention off the system behind the whole thing.

Last night there was a young pregnant woman on my local channel 10 station that had COVID and I think she was six weeks pregnant and she didn't get the shot because it frightened her, since we really don't know the long term effects and not really knowing for sure the safety with the rapid way its been rolled out as an experiment. She was speaking out though because she thought she should not be condemned and people treating her badly because of her choice not to get the shot. She told about how she had gone to Urgent Care after she realized she had COVID and when she got there the first thing they asked her was very bluntly; did you get the Shot? When she told them no and why, they said then she deserved or that's why you have COVID and REFUSED to treat her and sent her away. Now really folks, is this how we want our medical facilities to practice medical care? What if this was your daughter and even though you had encouraged her to get the shot, she didn't, out of the same fear as this woman had. Her own OBGYN believed as she did, that it was her choice and did not try to sway her either way. In this example it is so clear to me, we should not be beating up on each other. What is worse here, I believe and could be wrong, is the SYSTEM that refused her medical care is worse behavior than the young pregnant woman not getting the shot because of fear. Mandating and forcing people to do anything just doesn't work. Instead of us focusing on who did or did not get the shot and hating either of them that you've been told to by the media, focus on the systems behind this all and shine the light on that. Just like the food industry's drastic, healthy, organic changes over the past ten years, we can change what we stand up to together and say NO to in an intelligent way and non-violent manner. The system that turned this pregnant young woman away with no treatment, is to me much more of a hazard to our community than someone who doesn't want to get vaccinated. And, it's not the employees fault. It is their training and what they are being taught to believe is their job. And, as you probably know if you are 55 and over, doing your job is vital as well as doing what you are told. Another brainwashing we received.

Poliovirus was also very contagious and spread through person to person contact. I lived during the worst time for polio and I did take the vaccine. I faintly remember and I think I drank it from a cup. Since 1979, there are no known cases of polio in the United States contributing to the very effective vaccine. No one was forced to get vaccinated nor would anyone think to blame others if they didn't get vaccinated or better yet, they would have never told someone they deserved getting it, if they had not been vaccinated. I also read during the 1950's before the vaccination, it was the highest death rate and spread of polio and it said in the write up ,by a major medical institution, that the rapid spread of polio and thus deaths, was due to the enormous fear of the public that caused the polio to spread so rapidly. Hopefully, by now you can at least begin to at least consider that it may be true and a contributing factor that fear attracts like a magnet and may be somewhat part of the cause of the COVID spread and now the Delta variant rapid spread. I think that is why so many of the businesses are mandating proof of vaccines to enter their establishment, because they are AFRAID if they don't do something fast they will be shut down again. They are being controlled just as much as we are.

The point of all this is again, just like the masks if we were not hearing on the 24 hour horror news stations the deaths and good and bad people and who to blame and mandating what we have to do and building up more and more divide, then even COVID may have not spread as quickly and wide without all the fear. Also, we may have just been happy to get the vaccination if we knew it was coming from a place like the Scientist that found the cure for polio, of wanting to just help people and save lives which it did and everyone didn't get the shot. I know Polio is not the same as COVID. I'm just using that as an example of the difference in the way society as a whole responded and got through it and accepted and was grateful for the vaccine and without the input from the media, were not blaming each other or fearing the vaccination. Oh, do I miss the Walter Cronkite reporting, no opinions and his sign off And, "that's the way it is". By the way, I learned from a very reputable person who worked for a major broadcasting company, that after WaterGate, there was something passed that allowed for what was called 'COMMENTARY'. You didn't have to prove anything, just say whatever you want, which overnight all these Commentary News Stations built their empires and reached and are controlling 85% of our nation.

In order to visit your favorite business or maybe even fly to see your family, you may be mandated to get the shot. Even though I am against the mandate, you still have a choice. It may be more important to go ahead and get it because your family or whatever it is you truly want is more important than keeping your stance on not getting the shot. Especially if it's principle and not fear, like the pregnant woman. So get the shot if you believe it will help you and for those who don't want to get it don't do it. You have the right to make decisions for your body. However, if you are in a position that you have to in order to keep your job and you can't quit, you can still voice your truth and say NO. However, if you don't want to leave your job or if you need proof of vaccination to travel to see your loved ones, then it may be prudent to get the shot and accept it without any fear or anger and believe with you whole heart and soul that your body will work and ensure nothing is harmful to you. And, hey, You may just get the placebo if you are holding love, especially for yourself, and no blame to anyone else. Then no-one has taken your power away. You are still in love and peace and your focus is on working with all of us together to change the systems behind all this control. If Viktor Frankl could do this in the concentration camps then you can do it with a shot. He lived to write the book Man's Search for Meaning which made him immortal!!!!

Thirteen
The End or the Beginning?

IT IS ENTIRELY your choice if you want to believe you are
at the end of your life, maybe it is. God/Universe/Source will
never take you without your consent. If you are ready to go
and really are ready and feel you have completed and learned
all that you were here for, and you tell God you are ready,
then it's very possible you will just pass on in your sleep.
However, after reading this book and doing some research
on your own and opening up to the infinite possibilities, you
may want to have a new beginning because the best is yet
to come. We were never taught to rely and choose what it is
we want or believe is true for us and know that will become

the reality for us. I think most of us realize whether from religion or those around us growing up, for me I learned in my religion that we had free will.

Although I really didn't know how that could work for me even when it looked like my choices were taken from me. Circumstances happen to us and we think we have no choice, when in fact we always have a choice. WE think people, situations happen to us when in reality what happens is we give away our power. No one really takes it away. What we see is people and situations taking control and there is no way they can take your power away unless you give it to them by being/feeling fearful, unworthy or incapable. We give our power away by thinking they know better, are much more powerful, smarter, wealthier, and we have to go along for our own survival. When in fact we know deep inside this isn't what we want and we just want to belong and go along with whatever we think is going to make us safe and others think is the best for us. No one knows what is best for you. You are the only one who knows what is best for you and that is why you have to first know who you are before you can know what is best for you. How can anyone else know you, let alone know what is best for you. The only way to know you and what is best for you is to EXPERIENCE you. and, the only way to experience you is to be with you and keep asking "Who am I"? "What Am I"? and be silent and see what comes up. We were taught to just do whatever we were told by adults and people in authority. We were not taught to question authority or say no, when we know there is something not right going on. We just learned to take it, don't complain and question. Look at all the abuse of the boys in the catholic schools. Again, it is so good this is all coming out since this and other, what seems like terrible things are coming out. And, just like things within us that we don't want to look at and face, are coming out to be dissolved. The Catholic Church is not all bad nor are what seems to be damaging corporations and establishments. It's just the humans in it that have been programmed to do what they are told and just being human we do make mistakes. We all do even when we do know better. The majority of beliefs though have been programmed into us and aren't even really us. Everything will be changing as we bring it forward and look at it, and define what we do want it to be and let it be dissolved for the new beauty and holiness to replace it.

Again, pay attention to your body. It will let you know when there are unresolved emotions and traumas that are lodged in your mind and need to be released. If only we could realize that everything that is causing us conflict, illness or worry is within us. The only thing outside is something that triggers that which was already inside us or it would not have triggered it. We attract everything according to our past and what memories, vows, traumas that are in our lives. If we had an abusive father, then we most likely keep finding ourselves in an abusive relationships and no matter how aware we are that we keep getting into these relationships and why, it still keeps happening until we reprogram that vow or belief in our subconscious that we CAN choose differently and choose a beautiful kind and loving partner and have a wonderful happy relationship. That has to be the predominant thought each day and wanting more than anything to change the thought that we choose that keeps bringing us jerks. Then we think how powerless we are and then decide not to be in any relationship. When all you have to do is just choose again to be in a healthy wonderful relationship and feel and believe it until the old belief dissolves. Which is usually some belief of unworthiness or powerless belief and something you made up on how you are going to control the situation to avoid getting hurt, which really is not causing you to avoid the hurt, instead is responsible for the hurt, over and over again. Again, if you are having any illness, chronic pain, anxiety and are not able to break the patterns of your life that keep coming up over and over, then I strongly recommend Brandy Gilmore, Phd and her programs and also listening to her Podcasts can be life transforming and she takes volunteers on the her show, maybe they will pick you!!!

The real work and change is done by you. It won't work until you realize it's you and your power within that makes the changes and only if you are ready to let go of the things that you have believed is keeping you safe and instead is what is actually causing your pain and suffering. Just learn it's a choice to think, feel whatever you want. If things aren't looking good outside in your reality, choose again to something that you WANT it to look like and your reality changes. AS Wayne Dyer always said ,"When you change the way you look at things, the things you look at change". How many times have you heard someone say after something was explained to them, "Oh, I never looked at it THAT way." Oprah always loved hearing people say that and she is so responsible for changing and expanding the consciousness of thousands, probably millions of us on this planet. She gave us so many different aspects, things and beliefs to look at differently and that we did. Even our lifelong beliefs about aging. Wow we don't have to age like our parents or grandparents and look at us now!!! 50 is the new 30!!! So, choose what you want to feel each day when you wake up, choose bliss and gratefulness to experience each day thanking God/ Universe for being exactly who you are and living right now in this vital important time on earth. And, then ask, "What am I here for and how may I serve? Then watch for the flood of divine intervention and serendipity. You WILL get an answer.

If only I could come up with the words that would penetrate through and give everyone the realization of how important and vital and urgent that LOVING YOURSELF, must be mastered in order for you and also people around you to totally heal, awaken and transcend. Imagine if everyone truly loved themselves and they had eliminated all guilt, shame, pain, anger, hate and all they had within them was love and constant joy and bliss. Do you really think they would be afraid, angry, fighting others when they knew no matter what is happening out there, they still remained at peace and in love ,which happens automatically.

We can't make laws to make us love one another which is exactly what has been happening. For God sakes, look at all the turmoil within families and the anger, separation over things that most don't even remember what caused the separation that has gone on for years. Do you think for one minute if the Government made a law that we start loving and giving our money to our estranged and conflicting family members or we would be fined or even arrested, that would solve everything and they would happily oblige? Would that work? If anything it gets worse and yet ,that is exactly what we did with Civil Rights. It is so sad that we had to have a Law to just be kind to each other. All it did was cause more anger and conflict and make a lot of attorneys and others rich when laws were broken, which was almost guaranteed. And, I am pretty sure there are systems and groups behind the scenes that wanted exactly that ,so again we would be separated. We know with our children and/or even our partners and other adults all we have to do is say DON'T DO THIS OR THAT, and it's almost guaranteed that's what they will do. Because we have free will and no one wants someone else to demand we do anything we haven't chosen; wouldn't it be so much easier if we just all together chose to see others as important as ourselves and treat them accordingly and tell the Government no thank you on the laws. In truth THEY are ourselves and whatever we do to another we do to ourselves. That is a spiritual truth that you may want to explore.

So, the answer is so simple. Just project out with every ounce of your being LOVE into EVERYTHING. And, in order to do that and change the world around you, you start by LOVING YOURSELF, so it can be projected outward. You can't give what you don't have.

Don't F- - - with love it's all there is, without it, we will not even exist as a human race and will become extinct. We ARE Love. Let's not be the generation who destroyed the earth and everything on it. Wouldn't you rather be part of the ones who are ascending and transitioning and evolving with a new earth? If so, learn to love and trust yourself so that others will trust you and transcend with you as they feel your vibration lifting them.

About the Author

SALLY RETIRED IN 2002 from the Corporate world in Upper Management. Three years ago, she enrolled and completed the curriculum and earned her Certification from Mary Morrissey as a DreamBuilder Life Coach and started her own coaching business. Sally has one daughter, three grandchildren and two great grandchildren. Sally at 78 years young, is delighted with her life in every aspect and looking forward to an extraordinary future due to the teachings in this book that she made a priority to Master as well as the decision to Serve God/Universe/The One Creator first. This is her first book. You can reach Sally for more information on one-on-one and group coaching and her online classes at www.SallyPreston.DreamBuilderCoach.com. Also, you may email her at SallyPreston@DreamBuilderCoach.com. Sally specializes in coaching those 55+the realization and proof, that it is never too late to live the life of your dreams and experience heaven on earth. Also, tune into her Podcast beginning in November, 2021. Sally Preston It's Never Too Late Show. Each week will be 40 minutes and each week will have a different theme. First week will be '' Sallyisms" Day where she will talk about the Health and Wellness teaching in this book and also have guests who are experts in their field. Second week, LET ME ENTERTAIN YOU featuring different artists, musicians, singers, comedians and even dancers. Third Week Health and Fitness Day, Yoga and other exercises that are easy to do at home also Healthy food prep and nutrition education. Fourth Week Open Mind Day new concepts and information to blow your mind. Be sure and send her an email at SallyPreston@DreamBuilderCoach.com so she can let you know when Podcast is up and running.

References/Sally's List to Enlightenment and Transformation.

THIS IS MY reference to the Best of the Best. Remember I have read 1,000's of books and have attended as many classes and have obtained several certifications, and to save you the years of research and study, these people are so far what I have found to be the Best of the Best in learning to love yourself and dissolve the past trauma lingering within you.

1. Jennifer McLean her book and training on "Spontaneous Transformation."

2. Get Your Shift Together, CD Training. Bruce Liipton, Phd and Dr. Joe Dispenza. Science of Personal and Global Transformation.
3. The Code of the Extraordinary Mind, Vichen Lakhiani
4. Mary Mannin Morrissey, books, classes and the DreamBuilder Coach Certification Program
5. Matt Kahn Books" Whatever Arises Love That" "Everything is Here to Help You" and "The Universe Always has a Plan".
6. The Artist's Way, Julia Cameron (You will love yourself just taking the time for taking this Course).
7. E 2 book , Pam Grout. Proofing to you your thoughts create your reality.
8. Anita Moorjani's books. " Dying to be Me" and "Sensitive is the new Strong."
9. Rikki Zimmermann online training , Six Principles
10. Book, "The Desire Factor", Christy Whitman
11. Music to Heal you, Karen Drucker
12. "You're Not Broken ", Book and Online course, Christopher Michael Duncan
13. Brandy Gillmore, Classes and Podcast Heal Yourself. Change Your Life
14. And, ABSOLUTELY ANYTHING FROM WAYNE DYER.
15. Marianne Williamson, Book" Return to Love "and her courses on Course of Miracles.

This is not by far all the great genius that is out there and that I have read and followed for years. For example, I love

Depak Chopra and he is responsible for the beginning of my journey into the spiritual and scientific world. All the above are those that pertain to the teachings in this book, and who helped me in this specific area on my journey.

One book that doesn't exactly fit in with the above criteria of learning to love yourself and/or releasing trauma is authored by someone I love. Rania Lababidy's book "Tap into Miracles" A Reminder. It's a delightful book and easy to read and can empower you to live your truth, remember your natural creativity, magnetize to you all your good, and discover the importance of intuition.